got style?

A Fiction Writer's Companion

Helen Hardt

got style?

A Fiction Writer's Companion

This book is an original publication of Helen Hardt

The publisher does not assume any responsibility for third-party websites or their content.

Paperback ISBN: 0990746127
ISBN-13: 978-0-9907461-2-6

PRINTED IN THE UNITED STATES OF AMERICA

HS
HARDT & SONS ♥

Praise for Helen Hardt

I had no idea how much I didn't know about the fundamentals of fiction writing until my search for an editor for my first novel brought me to Helen. Her insights are thorough and to the point, but always thoughtful. As an established author, she brings both sensitivity and experience to the process, while challenging me to grow as a writer and improve my craft. At the end of the day, I can't imagine entrusting anyone else to help me bring my books across the finish line, from stories I've nursed on my own for months to completed works I can be proud to share with the world.

–Meredith Wild, #1 *New York Times* Bestselling Author of The Hacker Series

Helen is an outstanding editor who recognizes ways to make a writer's words shine while respecting that it is his voice, his characters, and his story. She taught me about problems with my writing that no previous editor had found, and she helped make my book an award winner! I look forward to working with her again as she launches her editing, and I highly recommend her.

–Deborah Schneider, 2011 EPIC Award Winner, 2009 RWA Librarian of the Year

When my editor Helen Hardt left commercial publishing to concentrate on her own career as author and freelance editor, I thought my heart would break. She's not only extremely knowledgeable in grammar, syntax, structure (all the classroom stuff), and purging unneeded verbiage, but she's also gifted at sensing how to strengthen emotion, in my opinion one of a romance novel's most important areas. Ironically, what Helen taught me and assisted me with can't be put into words. I just know it showed up on the pages of the books we did together and I hope her talents are evident in the works I've done since then.

–**Tanya Hanson**, 2011 Double CAPA Award Nominee

Helen, all your suggestions proved most helpful. Your keen eye spotted numerous areas where I hadn't maximized the emotional potential of a scene, so crucial in keeping the reader riveted to the story. Adding to that is your impressive mastery of the English language, to polish the work and catch mistakes which other editors missed. Your professional and friendly approach throughout made it a real treat in every way. Finally, you exhibit what some editors falter upon: you actually "walk the walk" in respecting the author's voice and style and working with the story's intent.

–Gary Weibert, Author

Helen educated me better than any MFA professor did, better than even my most trusted mentors and advisers in the past. Her nuts and bolts support and challenges have definitely taught me so much and made me more confident in myself in ways that will significantly impact my future writing.

–Callie Chase, Kindle Vella Bestselling Author of *Bug*

If you dream of writing a book and "getting it out there," Helen Hardt is just the person you need to help you achieve that dream. Helen is able to "see the big picture" of your story and envision the best way to develop the plot and characters. She really understood what I was trying to do in my writing and offered sound suggestions that I could use. Helen Hardt is a true professional!

–Cheryl Pierson, 2010 EPIC Finalist

To all the talented authors who have trusted me with their manuscripts, thank you. I learn something new with every edit.

Special thanks to Meredith Wild, Callie Chase, and Sloane Taylor, who have given me so much in return. You ladies rock!

Acknowledgements

I want to thank my mother, Elise Tom, who was a teacher of English and French. When I was in school, I never understood why people did so poorly in grammar. The correct answer was easy to spot. It was the one that sounded right. It didn't dawn on me until later in life that the reason the right answer sounded right to me was because I'd grown up hearing grammar used correctly. So thank you, Mom.

Two of my high school teachers—whom I mention later in this book—were grammar nerds like I am, and I owe two of my chapter names to them. Mrs. Lucy Coney and Mrs. Cheryl Vornbrock, wherever you are, I hope you are happy and in a good place.

Contents

Introduction

got grammar?

I admit up front that the name of this book is a bit of a misnomer. It is about style, yes, but it's also about grammar. Frankly, I didn't think anyone would actually buy a book called *got grammar?* I may be the only person in the free world who actually enjoys grammar. Nope, style sounds much more exciting. But to have good writing style, you must also have good grammar. That's not to say that every style issue is a grammar issue; many are not. But good grammar is as essential to good writing style as egg whites are to chocolate mousse. So I'm going to touch on a lot of grammar in this book. After all, no one wants to read a paragraph full of showing rather than telling if it's replete with grammatical errors. Not everyone is a grammar geek like I am, but let's face it. If you want to be a professional writer, you need to know the rules of your language.

"But that's my editor's job!"

No, it's your job. I can guarantee you that your editor is overworked and probably underpaid. The first thing he or she will ask when looking at your submission is, "How much work is this going to be for me to edit?" The story may be unique and amazing, but if the writing is a mess that will require hours upon hours upon hours of harrowing work, the editor will pass. Submitting a clean and well-crafted manuscript is your best chance of getting published.

"But I self-publish, so that scenario doesn't apply to me."

Au contraire, writing clean is even more important if you self-publish, especially if you choose to forego professional editing—which I don't recommend. Since self-publishing became the rage, a rash of poorly written books have been thrust upon innocent readers. If you want yours to stand out, it has to be great. After all, you don't want a grammar geek like me going at it with a mental red pen.

Okay, off the soapbox.

This book was born of my writing workshops on grammar and style. I wasn't kidding about the mental red pen. Ask any editor; it's nearly impossible not to correct as you read. I began to notice certain errors that were very common in published work—dangling modifiers, cumulative v.

coordinate adjective errors, transitive v. intransitive verb errors, to name a few. Don't know what those are? We'll get to that. Anyway, it occurred to me that not only are a lot of authors uneducated in some of the finer nuances of grammar and style, but some editors are too. It's impossible to know everything about English. Languages constantly evolve, and very few grammar and style rules are absolute. But hopefully this book will help both authors and editors—and anyone else who's interested—re-learn some of the finer points that have been long forgotten from English class.

Make no mistake. This book is not a substitute for *The Chicago Manual of Style* or any other good grammar reference. I'm including only those areas where I continually see errors in published work.

So in the same vein as two of my idols, William Strunk, Jr. and E.B. White of *The Elements of Style* (which should be on every writer's bookshelf), I'm making this a short but educational little volume. As the bard himself said, "Brevity is the soul of wit."

Let's get some style.

I

To Be or not To Be

This poor little verb has gotten a bad rap. Yes, "to be" is the weakest verb in English. However, it exists for a reason. Some writers and editors want to avoid "to be" at all costs, kind of like taking four right turns to avoid that left turn you really aren't comfortable making.

But you know what? Sometimes things just "are."

It's not a bad idea, though, to search your completed manuscript for forms of "to be" and eliminate any that you can.

Do a search for the following—

be

is

am

are

was

were

been

being

This list should catch all of the instances of "to be" no matter what the tense. Take a look at each instance and see if a better way exists to show what you want to say.

Here are a few examples of what may come up during your search.

Eliminate past progressive tense.

She was walking. As opposed to simple past— *She walked.*

Is showing the action in progress necessary? Sometimes it is, but more often than not, simple past can be substituted without changing the meaning of your sentence.

Turn the subjective complement into a verb.

J.K. Rowling is the writer of the Harry Potter series.

Becomes—

J.K. Rowling wrote the Harry Potter series.

Eliminate passive voice.

She was terrified by the thunderstorm.

Becomes—

The thunderstorm terrified her.

Turn an adjective into a verb.

The game was exciting.

Becomes—

The game excited him.

Eliminate expletives.

"F*** that noise!"

Nope, not that kind of expletive. I'm talking about expletive constructions.

English has two expletive words: there and it.

Don't confuse the expletive it with the referential it. The latter is a pronoun with a clear antecedent. The expletive it has no referent.

For example—

The boy threw the ball, and the dog caught it.

The it has a clear antecedent, *ball*. This is a referential it, not an expletive it.

It was when the doorbell rang that I realized I wasn't ready.

The it has no referent and is therefore expletive.

To the same end, don't confuse the expletive there with the adverbial there. The latter is an adverb and acts as a modifier.

Adverbial there—

He placed the book there.

Expletive there—

There was a crash of thunder.

Too many expletives weaken writing. Rewrite such sentences concentrating on precise action verbs and picture nouns. The two examples can easily be rewritten without expletives.

I wasn't ready when the doorbell rang.

Thunder crashed through the air.

II

Comma On

The poor little comma is underused, overused, and everything in between. The comma signals a brief pause and is often necessary to prevent misreading. The new thought in fiction writing is to eliminate commas where they're not needed for comprehension. This helps keep the read smooth. Most authors know the basics, but here are some areas where I still find many errors.

Direct Address

Use a comma to set off names of people spoken to in direct address.

Mom, I need to talk to you.

I understand, honey, but we still need to get to the store today.

Coordinate Adjectives (v. Cumulative Adjectives)

Coordinate adjectives are two adjectives in a row that each modify the noun equally (as opposed to cumulative adjectives, where the one next to the noun modifies the noun, and the other modifies the combination formed by the closer adjective and the noun.) Coordinate adjectives are separated by commas. Cumulative adjectives are *not* separated by commas.

For further discussion, see Section XIV.

Introductory Transitional Phrases

Use a comma after introductory transitional phrases such as "in fact," "as a result," and "on the other hand."

On the contrary, I thought the movie had a lot of merit.

Introductory Participial Phrases and Absolute Constructions (a noun plus a participial phrase)

Use a comma after a participial phrase or absolute construction at the beginning of a sentence.

Brushing my hair, I hummed to myself.

Her palm pressed against her cheek, she stared at the handsome man.

Introductory Infinitive Phrases

A comma must follow an introductory infinitive phrase.

To encourage good behavior, the teacher began using a points system.

Commas with Clauses of Attribution in Dialogue

Insert a comma between a clause of attribution and dialogue. The clause of attribution can appear at the beginning, middle, or end of a sentence. (If the clause of attribution occurs at the end of the sentence, an exclamation point or question mark can be used instead of a comma if the sentence calls for it.)

She said, "I wish I were going."

"I wish I were going," she said.

"I wish I were going," she said, "but we can't afford it."

Commas Following Yes or No

A comma should follow "yes," "no," and similar terms.

Yes, I would like to go along.

Commas Setting off Nonrestrictive Appositives

An appositive is a noun or noun phrase that provides additional information about another noun. A restrictive appositive restricts the meaning of the word or words immediately preceding it. A restrictive element must never be set off with any form of punctuation. On the contrary, a nonrestrictive appositive provides extra information that is not crucial to the meaning of the sentence and must be set off by commas. *Extra information equals extra commas.*

For further discussion, see Section XIII.

Discretionary Use of Comma

The Oxford Comma

I'm a firm believer in the Oxford or serial comma. The Oxford comma in a series avoids ambiguity and aids clarity.

You've no doubt seen the image on Facebook showing JFK and Stalin dressed in lingerie above this sentence: *We invited the strippers, JFK and Stalin.*

Had the writer used the Oxford comma, the sentence would have read correctly: *We invited the strippers, JFK, and Stalin.*

I have no idea what type of event would feature JFK, Stalin, and strippers, but that's not really the point. The point is that JFK and Stalin are not strippers (at least not that we know of) and without the Oxford comma, the sentence reads as though they are.

That being said, both sentences are considered correct by today's standards. Not by my personal standards, but by the English language speaking public in general. My advice? Use the Oxford comma. It is always correct. The only time I'd advise avoiding it is when it goes against your publisher's house style, which it sometimes does.

Commas in Compound Sentences

A compound sentence is two independent clauses joined by a coordinating conjunction. Historically, all such sentences required a comma before the conjunction. Today, whether a comma is used is up to the author or editor, especially if the two independent clauses are short and well balanced. The following are both considered correct.

He threw the ball and the dog caught it.

He threw the ball, and the dog caught it.

Introductory Adverbs

A comma is usually used after an adverb at the beginning of a sentence, but it can be discretionary if a pause is not necessary.

Surprisingly, he decided to run for office.

Then he heard a loud scream.

Actually she went with them.

Commas Before Too

When "too" is used as an adverb, a comma is discretionary. Most of the time sentences go right along without a needed pause, and the fewer pauses in your writing, the more fluid the read.

However, a comma can be used if you want to emphasize an abrupt change of thought. To illustrate—

"I had cake," Tommy said.

"I had cake too," Ellen said.

No abrupt change of thought there. However—

"I had ice cream for dessert," Tommy said. "What did you have?"

"I had ice cream," Ellen said, "and I had cake, too."

III

Getting Tense

Most fiction is written in past tense, though more authors—think Suzanne Collins and E.L. James—are using present tense for narrative today. Whatever tense you choose to write in, make sure your tenses are sequenced correctly. For example, when writing in past tense and relating an incident that happened before the narrative, use past perfect tense. However, if you're using present tense for your narrative, simple past should be used for an event that happened previous to the narrative.

I'm going to make this easier by taking you through all of the verb tenses in English and how to use them. I'll use the same sentence for each example: *I walk to work.*

Present Tenses

Simple present—this is happening now or is habit.

I walk to work.

Present progressive—this is happening now, as you are reading this.

I am walking to work.

Present perfect—this began sometime in the past and continues now.

I have walked to work for the past six months.

Past Tenses

Simple past—this happened in the past and is not presently happening.

I walked to work yesterday.

Past progressive—this happened while something else happened.

I was walking to work when my cell phone rang.

Past perfect—this happened before another occurrence in the past.

I had walked to work for a week before I broke my leg.

Past perfect progressive—this was happening when something happened to stop it.

I had been walking to work for a week, and then I broke my leg.

Future Tenses

Simple future—this hasn't happened yet.

I will walk to work tomorrow.

Future progressive—this hasn't happened yet, but will be happening when something else happens.

I will be walking to school tomorrow when the bus comes.

Future perfect—this will happen in the future before something else happens.

I will have walked to school for three days when Grandma gets here next week.

Future perfect progressive—this will be happening in the future when something else happens.

I will have been walking to school for three days by next Friday.

Conditional Tenses

Present conditional—something will happen if something else happens.

If the sun is out, I will walk to school tomorrow.

Past conditional—if something were happening, something else would be happening.

If the sun were out, I would walk to school.

Perfect conditional—if something had happened, something else would have happened.

If the sun had been out, I would have walked to school.

Note— While present conditional refers to something that will or might happen, both past and perfect conditional refer to situations that will not happen.

Errors in Tense Sequencing

The most common tense sequencing error occurs in narrative when you're relating an event in the past to another event further in the past. Use the simple past tense to relate the first event and the past perfect tense for the event further in the past.

Incorrect— *I told him I was calling because I was in a play several years ago.*

Correct— *I told him I was calling because I had been in a play several years ago.*

Another common error is the use of a perfect infinitive with the conditional perfect tense.

Incorrect— *Tricia would have preferred to have stayed with Edward.*

Correct— *Tricia would have preferred to stay with Edward.*

And the third most common sequencing error is using the future conditional to show both the condition and the result had the condition been met rather than past perfect plus future conditional.

Incorrect— *If I would have been there, I would have sung.*

Correct— *If I had been there, I would have sung.*

Are you tense yet? That wasn't so difficult, was it? Tenses and sequencing become second nature once you understand the purpose of each form.

Relax!

IV

This Chapter Will Be Read By You

And that, my friends, is passive voice. Passive voice occurs when the subject of the sentence (in this case, the chapter) is being acted upon rather than doing the acting.

The ball was thrown by Jim.

The boy was bitten by the dog.

Passive voice is formed by taking the correct form of the verb "to be" plus the past participle of the action verb.

During my editing career, I've encountered a lot of myths about passive voice. For example, many would say the following is passive voice.

I was walking to the gym.

Nope, not passive voice. That is past progressive tense, and yes, it uses a form of "to be" to show that the action is occurring even as we speak. Wordy, yes, and simple past can often be substituted without changing the meaning: *I walked to the gym.*

But it's not passive voice. The subject (I) is doing the acting. That's active voice.

Myth number one busted— Past progressive tense is not passive voice.

During my grammar and style workshops, when I ask the attendees where the grammatical error is in a sentence, often someone points to passive voice. Nope. Passive voice is perfectly grammatically correct; it's just not always the optimal way to show the action.

Myth number two busted— Passive voice is not a grammatical error.

Often people think that any use of "to be" constitutes passive voice. As noted previously, "to be" is generally a weak verb, and oftentimes better ways exist to show your meaning, but "to be" doesn't automatically mean passive voice.

Myth number three busted— Using "to be" does not automatically mean passive voice.

In general, passive voice should be avoided. And I just used passive voice in that sentence, which segues nicely into when passive voice is appropriate. You might use it in the following cases.

The actor is not known.

The playground was vandalized.

The actor is not important.

A new shopping center will be built on the southwest corner of Main and High Streets.

You don't want to mention who the actor is (common in mystery writing).

Blood was smeared on the doorknob.

V

And Two More Myths Busted

Two rules you probably learned in school actually have no basis in today's grammar rules.

First, never begin a sentence with a coordinating conjunction. You may have noticed as you've been reading that I've begun several sentences with coordinating conjunctions. The technique is perfectly acceptable and is useful for emphasis. But like all techniques, it's best used sparingly, or the emphasis will be lost.

Re-read the previous sentence. You'll see that it begins with a coordinating conjunction (but), which works well.

Here's a quick mnemonic device for the coordinating conjunctions: FANBOYS.

F—for

A—and

N—nor

B—but

O—or

Y—yet

S—so

Second, you were probably taught never to end a sentence with a preposition. Though it is best avoided, especially in formal writing, sometimes it's necessary. Take a look at the following.

What are you looking at?

"At" is a preposition, and according to many ancient English teachers, this sentence is *verboten*. However, take a look at the alternative.

At what are you looking?

Okay, who speaks like this? Really? This rule is a myth, no doubt invented by a pretentious teacher long ago.

VI

Congratulations, Did You Take Feeling Lessons?

Basic grammar was required for freshmen at my high school. My teacher, Mrs. Cheryl Vornbrock, was teaching us about adjectives and adverbs when the whole good v. well debacle came up.

"You've always been taught to say 'I feel well,'" she said, "but since well is an adverb, and you're describing yourself, an adverb isn't correct. An adverb would correctly modify the verb, which is "to feel."

So, Mrs. Vornbrock advised, "when someone tells you, 'I feel well,' say, 'Congratulations, did you take feeling lessons?'"

With all due respect to Mrs. Vornbrock, the situation isn't quite so simple. In this case, "to feel" is not an action verb but a linking verb. Linking verbs communicate a state of being as opposed to an action. They "link" words together, and are sometimes called "copulative verbs." So just imagine them joining two words together to have sex or copulate.

The most common linking verb is, of course, "to be," but others that can function as linking verbs include, but are not limited to, "to feel," "to seem," "to become," and "to appear," as well as sensory verbs like "to smell" or "to taste." The noun or adjective that follows the linking verb is the subjective complement. In other words, it completes the thought and identifies the subject.

She seems happy.

He is the president of the club.

Mom feels depressed.

Dad became the coach when Grandpa retired.

Tom is good at running. (Not *Tom is well at running.*)

Some linking verbs can also be used as action verbs. Take a look at these two sentences.

Bob smells good.

Bob smells well.

The first sentence means that Bob has been using his deodorant regularly and maybe he put on some aftershave. Smell is a linking verb, and good is the subjective complement. The second sentence means Bob is really good at smelling and is perhaps descended from dogs. Smell is an action verb, and well is an adverb modifying smell.

To decide whether the verb in a sentence is used as an action verb (in which case you'd use an adverb to describe the action) or a linking verb (in which case you'd use an adjective to describe the subject), see if you can substitute "to be" for the verb. If you can, and the sentence still makes sense, the verb is a linking verb.

Many of us have been taught since we were knee high to say "I feel well" rather than "I feel good." That isn't going to disappear and will probably always be considered correct by many. But hold your head high and say "I feel good." If someone corrects you, remind him that when you're happy, you say "I feel happy," not "I feel happily."

And when someone tells you he feels well, say, "Congratulations, did you take feeling lessons?"

VII

The Semicolon; Just Say No

Did you notice the semicolon error in my chapter heading? If not, read on.

Throughout the years, authors and editors have accused me of hating the semicolon. Not so. I don't hate this tiny punctuation mark. I do, however, hate the *misuse* of the semicolon.

This little mark is among the most misused in English. I encourage authors and editors not to use it in fiction at all. It's easily avoided. However, if you're bound and determined to use it, here's how to do it right.

The semicolon is a divider. It is used only to separate grammatically parallel elements. It separates independent clauses in compound and compound-complex sentences and separates items in a series when one or more of the items include interior punctuation.

Correct—

His stomach said he was hungry; his head reminded him of his goal to lose weight. (Two independent clauses joined.)

He begged her to stay; however, she left on the train at noon. (Two independent clauses joined by a conjunctive adverb.)

My favorite movies are Titanic; Yours, Mine, and Ours; and Avatar. (A series of three items, one of which includes interior punctuation.)

Any other use of the semicolon is incorrect.

So just say no.

With correct use of the period, comma, and em dash, the semicolon can easily be avoided.

VIII

Irritable Colon

Though I've used both the semicolon and colon throughout this non-fiction manual, no reason exists to use either in fiction. They look out of place and are disruptive to the reader. I advise against them, but if you do use them, please use them correctly.

The colon is an introducer. It introduces something like a list, clarification, or example. The sentence preceding the colon must be an independent clause.

All authors are taught one important principle: editors must be treated with respect.

He is an expert in four varietals of wine: Merlot, Pinot Noir, Chardonnay, and Riesling.

The colon is rarely seen in fiction.

IX

Dangling Around

Misplaced Modifiers

A misplaced modifier is a word, phrase, or clause that is erroneously separated from the word it modifies or describes. This can be corrected by changing the order of the words in the sentence. For example—

They saw a tub behind the house made of cast iron.

Is the house made of cast iron? Probably not, but that's what this sentence says. Correct it by moving "made of cast iron."

They saw a tub made of cast iron behind the house.

Dangling Modifiers

A dangling modifier is a phrase or clause that seems to modify a word but in reality is not logically related to the word. This *cannot* be corrected by changing the order of the words in the sentence. It requires a rewrite.

Walking to the grocery store, the rain drenched Marie.

What the author means to say here is that Marie got drenched while walking to the store. What the author is actually saying is that the rain was walking to the store. Rewrite the sentence.

Rain drenched Marie while she walked to the grocery store.

You could also say:

Walking to the grocery store, Marie got drenched by rain.

But this results in passive voice, which is best avoided in fiction.

After cumulative v. coordinate adjective errors, dangling modifiers are the errors I see most frequently in published fiction. Your best defense is to learn to spot them from a mile away and to learn the following strategies for revising them.

Name the appropriate actor as the subject of the main clause

Having missed the deadline, the paper was late to the printer.

Who missed the deadline? This sentence says that the paper missed the deadline, which is impossible since a paper is an inanimate object. To revise, decide who actually missed the deadline.

Having missed the deadline, John caused the paper to be late to the printer.

The main clause now names the person who did the action in the modifying phrase.

Change the dangling phrase into a complete introductory clause by naming the actor of the action in that clause

Because John missed the deadline, the paper was late to the printer.

The phrase is now a complete introductory clause; it does not modify any other part of the sentence, so it isn't dangling.

Combine the phrase and main clause into a simple or compound sentence

John missed the deadline, and the paper was late to the printer.

X

Lay This Down While I Lie Here

I'm still amazed how many times I see these two little verbs misused in published work. Admittedly, their conjugation can be confusing. The past tense of "to lie" is the present tense of "to lay," for example. I promise, though, once you learn the difference between a transitive and an intransitive verb and memorize the forms, you'll never confuse them again.

A transitive verb is one that requires a direct object. "To lay" is a transitive verb. You lay something on the table, but you don't lay down. You can lay another person down (physically, you're laying him on the bed) but you yourself cannot lay down, nor can you tell another person to lay down. Yes, I'm sorry, but Eric Clapton is grammatically incorrect when he commands Sally to *lay* down.

To the contrary, an intransitive verb is a verb that has no object. To lie is such a verb. To die and to sleep are other examples of intransitive verbs.

You can't sleep someone or die someone or something. You and you alone can only sleep or die yourself. You also can't lie something. You can only lie down yourself.

Now that you know which verb to use, let's look at their forms. This gets sticky for some people because they've said it wrong for so long, the correct form doesn't sound right to them. Trust me, you'll get used to it.

Broken down, here are the forms.

To lay

present tense—lay

past tense—laid

past participle—laid

To lie

present tense—lie

past tense—lay

past participle—lain (this is the one that seems to freak people out)

Let's put them into action.

Today I lie down.

Yesterday I lay down.

For the past three weeks, I have lain down for a nap each afternoon.

Today I lay the pencil on the table.

Yesterday I laid the pencil on the table.

For the past three weeks, I have laid a pencil on the table every afternoon.

"To sit" and "to set" are another example of an intransitive/transitive combo. "To sit" is intransitive. You can sit down, but you can't sit something down. To the contrary, you set something down. These two are much easier to conjugate.

Today I sit down.

Yesterday I sat down.

For the past three weeks, I have sat down each afternoon.

Today I set the pencil on the table.

Yesterday I set the pencil on the table.

For the past three weeks, I have set the pencil on the table.

Just remember the difference between transitive and intransitive verbs, and I promise you'll never "lay" down for a nap again.

XI

I'm in a Subjunctive Mood Today

Believe it or not, the English language has moods too. The mood is simply the quality of a verb that makes the sentence a statement, a question, a command, or a conjecture.

The indicative mood refers to a statement of fact and can be in any tense.

I *went* to the movies.

We *will go* tomorrow.

The interrogative mood refers to a question and can be in any tense.

Did you *remember* your purse?

What *are* you doing?

The imperative mood refers to a command or order. It is always in the present tense and takes the infinitive form.

Set the table.

Be a good boy.

Have a nice day.

Pretty straightforward up to this point. But here's the tricky one.

The subjunctive mood refers to the expression of wishes, contingencies, conjectures, desires, recommendations, or anything else contrary to fact, and can be in present or past tense. This is where I see a lot of mistakes in published work.

If I *were* you, I'd go on the trip.

I wish she *were* able to go.

He asked that she *be* informed of the itinerary.

The office requires that an employee *update* his calendar regularly.

The subjunctive usually shows up with the verb "to be," but can show up with other verbs. For verbs other than "to be," the subjunctive is formed by using the infinitive form for all subjects. This usually only changes for third person singular, as it drops the "s" on those forms.

I asked that she *stop* speaking, but she didn't.

For the verb "to be," the infinitive form "be" is used for present tense, and "were" is used for past. See the examples above.

Caveat— When the word "if" is followed by the verb "to be," the mood is not automatically subjunctive. Make sure it is conjecture. For example—

He paused to see if she was waiting.

This sentence requires indicative mood, not subjunctive. He's not wishing she were waiting, or assuming. He doesn't know, and he's pausing to find out. Therefore, not subjunctive, but indicative.

With some practice, these will become second nature. So get your subjunctive on!

And the previous sentence is in the imperative mood.

XII

Which That is Which?

Authors are often encouraged to get rid of "that" when it's not necessary. In these cases, the "that" is an extra word that is unnecessary to the meaning of the sentence. You're not replacing "that" with another word. For example—

He knew that the day was ending.

The "that" here is an unnecessary word. You can just as easily say:

He knew the day was ending.

However, when "that" is used as a relative pronoun, it has a purpose in the sentence. Sometimes editors and authors confuse the relative pronoun "that" with the relative pronoun "which."

Use "that" with restrictive clauses and "which" with non-restrictive clauses. Non-restrictive clauses are usually set off by commas. A restrictive clause is essential to the meaning of the sentence. A nonrestrictive clause can be removed without changing the meaning of the sentence.

Let's take a look at the sentence in my first paragraph above.

In these cases, the "that" is an extra word that is unnecessary to the meaning of the sentence.

This is a restrictive clause. We're talking specifically about "that." Let's look at the same sentence using which.

In these cases, the "that" is an extra word, which is unnecessary to the meaning of the sentence.

The clause is now non-restrictive, which means it can be deleted and the sentence has the same meaning. (Incidentally, the previous sentence also contains a non-restrictive clause.) This sentence says simply that "that" is an extra word, and implies that all extra words are unnecessary to the meaning of the sentence. Obviously that's not what we want to say here.

XIII

Jane Doe is the only Bestselling Author in the Universe

How many of you have read an author bio that begins something like this?

Bestselling author, Jane Doe, began writing as a child.

I see this all the time, so it may surprise some of you to learn that the commas setting off "Jane Doe" are incorrect.

"Jane Doe" is a restrictive appositive in this sentence. An appositive is a noun or noun phrase that renames or provides further information about another noun.

A restrictive appositive is crucial to the meaning of the sentence. A nonrestrictive appositive is not. A nonrestrictive appositive is extra information and therefore is set off in the sentence by commas.

In the sentence above, the commas indicate that "Jane Doe" is a nonrestrictive appositive, meaning you could take out "Jane Doe" and the meaning of the sentence would still be the same.

The best-selling author began writing as a child.

This sentence assumes that everyone knows who it refers to—that only one bestselling author exists and there's no reason to name him. This means that Jane Doe is the only best-selling author in the known universe! Dan Brown, Nora Roberts, and J.K. Rowling might beg to differ, as might some of you.

The sentence becomes correct after removing the commas.

Bestselling author Jane Doe began writing as a child.

Use the commas when the information is not crucial to the sentence. For example, if we assume the current president of the United States is a person named Laura Doe and one of the previous presidents is a person named Harvey Doe—

The President of the United States, Laura Doe, is visiting a high school in Chicago.

There is only one president, so if we took out "Laura Doe," the meaning of the sentence would not change. Therefore, it's extra information and requires extra commas.

However, if we change the sentence—

The former President Harvey Doe is speaking at a high school in Chicago.

Now we don't need the commas because there is more than one former president alive today. If we took out "Harvey Doe," we'd have no way of knowing which president was going to speak.

Here's another example. Let's assume I have one brother and his name is Tom. The following is correct.

My brother, Tom, is coming for a visit.

Since I have only one brother, the sentence could only refer to Tom, so if we take Tom out, the sentence still has the same meaning.

My brother is coming for a visit.

Now, let's assume I have two brothers, Tom and Jim. We need to remove the commas.

My brother Tom is coming for a visit.

"Tom" is necessary information in this sentence, not extra information. Without "Tom," the reader doesn't know which brother I'm talking about.

Remember— extra information equals extra commas.

XIV

She Wore Her Leather, Black Pants

Coordinate adjectives are two adjectives in a row that each modify the noun equally, as opposed to cumulative adjectives, where the one closer to the noun modifies the noun, and the other modifies the combination formed by the closer adjective and the noun. Coordinate adjectives are separated by commas. Cumulative adjectives are *not* separated by commas.

This is the single most common mistake I find in published fiction.

To tell whether the adjectives are cumulative or coordinate, use the following tests.

Does the sentence still make sense if you reverse the adjectives? If so, the adjectives are coordinate and must be separated by a comma.

Does the sentence still make sense if you insert "and" between the two adjectives? If so, the adjectives are coordinate and must be separated by a comma.

The adjectives must pass *both* of the tests to be coordinate. If they pass only one or neither, they are cumulative and are not separated with a comma.

Let's take a look at this chapter heading.

She wore her leather, black pants.

I purposely reversed these two adjectives and inserted an incorrect comma. You probably noticed it right away, because no one would say "leather black pants." You'd say "black leather pants." These are classic cumulative adjectives, and a comma between them is an error. Let's apply the tests.

Can these two adjectives be separated with "and"?

She wore her leather and black pants.

She wore her black and leather pants.

Nope. The first sentence says she's wearing leather and she's wearing black pants, not that she's wearing black leather pants. The second says she's wearing black plus leather pants.

Can the two adjectives be reversed?

She wore her leather black pants.

Nope again. No one would ever say "leather black pants."

Consider these two sentences.

Jackie loves expensive, beautiful gowns.

Jackie loves expensive designer gowns.

In the first sentence, the two adjectives are coordinate and require a comma. You can easily apply the two tests and the sentence still makes sense.

Jackie loves beautiful, expensive gowns.

Jackie loves expensive and beautiful gowns.

Now let's try the second sentence.

Jackie loves expensive and designer gowns.

Jackie loves designer, expensive gowns.

These are clearly coordinate adjectives. "Designer" modifies "gowns," and "expensive" modifies "designer gowns."

A certain order exists for cumulative adjectives, though there are exceptions. In general, though, if you follow this order you will probably be correct.

Determiner—a, the, some, a few, several

Observation—gorgeous, worn, expensive

Size—big, small, medium

Shape—long, oval, triangular

Age—old, antique, new

Color—black, gray, red, yellow

Origin—French, English, American

Material—cotton, leather, silk, gold, oak

Qualifier—football (team), cardboard (boxes)

Noun

Use the preceding order to determine where to place cumulative adjectives. Honestly, though, the easiest way is to use the two tests.

Occasionally you'll run across adjectives that seem to be on "the cusp" between cumulative and coordinate. Perhaps they pass one of the tests but not the other. In these cases, I recommend eliminating the comma and treating them as cumulative adjectives. Fewer commas in narrative makes for a smoother read.

And that is your ultimate goal—a smooth read that keeps your reader engaged.

XV

Dash it All!

The em dash and the ellipsis are useful in fiction, though they're often used incorrectly. Avoid using parentheses in fiction.

The Em Dash

The em dash indicates an interruption in speech or emphasis of a phrase.

The em dash has a typewriter history. In those days, it was represented by double hyphens amounting to the width of a capital M from the keyboard. With computers, you can format or insert an em dash easily, and it's used to indicate an interruption within dialogue or to emphasize a certain phrase.

We walked to the mall—the new one in Coral Gables—before dinner.

"I thought you were going to— Oh, forget it."

The em dash looks like this —. The em dash does not have a space before or after it (unless it occurs at the end of a sentence, in which case do not punctuate the end of the sentence other than the dash, but add a space before beginning the next sentence.) When it is used within a sentence, do not use spaces.

To make an em dash in Microsoft Word, press CTRL, ALT, and the dash above the number pad on the right side of the keyboard.

The Ellipsis

The ellipsis shows a pause within narrative or dialogue or missing text within quoted material.

The ellipsis is always three dots "…". Always three, no more and no less. You may have learned in typing class to add a fourth dot to signify the period at the end of the sentence. That is no longer standard. Now, use only three periods, whether your ellipsis is at the end of a sentence or not (unless your publisher's house style indicates otherwise).

Use an ellipsis with words trailing off.

"Yesterday, we went…"

"What? Where did you go?"

Ellipses are great for slowing the reader down within narrative.

Jared gazed at her, trailing his fingers over her skin smoothly…softly…like a whisper.

In addition, use an ellipsis to show missing text in quoted material.

Parentheses

Parentheses are not recommended in fiction unless they're part of a quotation or written correspondence. The main purpose of parentheses is to deemphasize something. In fiction, anything that needs de-emphasis doesn't need to be there. In the immortal words of Strunk and White, two of my personal heroes, "Omit needless words."

XVI

We are Plural, not Possessive!

If Mrs. Vornbrock of the "feeling lessons" fame was Obi-Wan Kenobi, Mrs. Lucy Coney, my expository composition teacher senior year in high school, was Yoda. Mrs. Coney was a tiny spitfire of a woman who quoted Thoreau and considered good grammar as essential as good nourishment— a sentiment she passed on to me.

While teaching the difference between plural and possessive, she told a story about a visit to some friends. Their plane was delayed, so she and her husband sent a telegram to their hosts. She dictated the following to the operator: *The Coneys will arrive at 5:15.*

The operator furrowed his brow at "Coneys," and Mrs. Coney, in her loud and authoritative voice, said, "C-O-N-E-Y-S. We are plural, not possessive!"

I bet that operator never made that particular mistake again. Alas, many others do. Most get the easy words right. How hard is it to write my dog's collar or my cat's ball of yarn? But I'll take you through the whole ball of wax, just so it's all clear.

Plural

Making singular nouns plural is pretty straightforward. For the most part, add "s" (or "es" if the noun ends in s) to the noun unless the noun has a plural that changes the word, such as child to children.

However, this gets tricky in a few places, most notably when a proper last name ends in s, such as Jones or Davis.

Never use an apostrophe to make these proper nouns plural.

Incorrect— *The Jones' have three daughters.*

Instead, use "es."

The Joneses have three daughters.

In general, do not use apostrophes to make anything plural.

The 1960s produced some great thinkers.

Have you sent out your RSVPs for the parties?

Melanie got three As and two Bs.

The only time an apostrophe should be used for a plural is when a sentence is unclear without it.

In church, all the thees and thous get frustrating.

Better— *In church, all the thee's and thou's get frustrating.*

Better yet— Rewrite the sentence to avoid having to use an apostrophe to form a plural.

Possessive

Use "apostrophe s" to make singular nouns possessive even when the word or name ends in s.

Texas's border is huge.

Charles's suit looks great.

My boss's daughter was in the office today.

Robby Jones's house is beautiful.

Caveat— If your publisher's house style uses only the apostrophe in this situation (and some do), follow that rule for that publisher.

When the word is plural and ends in s, use only the apostrophe without an additional s.

The Joneses' house is beautiful.

The kids' toys are expensive.

If the word is plural and does not end in s, use "apostrophe s."

The children's toys are expensive.

XVII

You Can Quote Me on That

Quotation Marks

Single quotation marks are only appropriate when you are writing a quote within a quote or a quote within dialogue. Single quotes are not used on their own when they are not contained within double quotes.

"What did she say to you, David?" Mark asked.

"She said, 'I want to break up,'" David said.

The Apostrophe

The apostrophe is used in contractions, possessives, and in very few plurals. An apostrophe also signifies missing letters in a word.

Do not confuse the apostrophe with the open single quote.

Consider the following.

'tis

'tis

The first is incorrect, the second, correct.

'Tis is a contraction of "it is," often seen in historical fiction. Microsoft Word makes this difficult because when we type an apostrophe at the beginning of a word, Word assumes we're starting a quotation and gives us an open single quote instead of an apostrophe (which is identical to a closed single quote.)

This isn't a problem when the apostrophe occurs in the middle of a word or the end of a word. To get an apostrophe at the beginning of a word, we have to trick Word.

When typing a word such as 'tis (or 'em or 'twas or 'cause, etc.), you must type the apostrophe twice.

''tis

Then go back and delete the first one, so that only the second and correct one remains.

'tis

When editing, place your cursor between the open quote and the first letter of the word. Type an apostrophe (Word thinks you're closing the quote, so you'll get the correct character), backspace over the apostrophe, and delete the open quote. This will become second nature to you once you do it a few times.

XVIII

He Said, She Said

I'm going to assume that you already know the basics of dialogue punctuation—use commas when setting off a dialogue tag (which indicates speech) and use periods when setting off an action beat (which indicates non-speaking action).

Often new authors make the mistake of using just about anything for a dialogue tag. A dialogue tag must denote speech. Sighed, breathed, winked, smiled, etc. are not dialogue tags and must be punctuated as action beats. However, verbs like sighed, breathed, laughed, etc. can be used as dialogue tags *if* the dialogue is brief enough that the character actually "sighed" it. I advise using these sparingly. Action beats are much more effective.

Let's get down to style in dialogue.

First, dialogue is a wonderful tool for "showing" as opposed to "telling." If written well, it's much more fun to read than a bunch of narrative, and it helps build characterization. Be sure to read your dialogue out loud to yourself to make sure it flows naturally.

Inner dialogue—the character's thoughts—are italicized and in first person present tense. Though restricted to the POV character, inner dialogue allows you to dig deep and eliminate the tedious "he thought" and "he wondered."

Dialogue tags are a necessary evil, but should be kept to a minimum. If it is easy to understand who is speaking, the dialogue tag is probably not necessary. Try to use only one dialogue tag per block of dialogue. Interrupting a paragraph of dialogue with multiple tags results in splintered writing.

If some indication of who is speaking is necessary, action beats are usually much stronger than dialogue tags. They "show" rather than "tell." For example—

"Leave me alone," she said.

"Leave me alone." She trembled and gripped the stem of her wine glass.

Which sentence gave you a clearer picture? Most likely the second one, which used an action beat instead of a dialogue tag.

When a dialogue tag is necessary, stick with basics like "he said" or "he asked." Though it may feel repetitive, the reader is trained to gloss over these words, and his read will be smoother.

Each person's dialogue should have its own separate paragraph. Keep other characters' thoughts and actions out of the speaking character's dialogue paragraph. Only the speaker should be thinking and acting in his own dialogue paragraph. If someone else is doing something, start a new paragraph. This eliminates confusion and aids comprehension.

In addition, if your character is speaking and changes the subject to the point where you need to begin a new paragraph, do not put a quotation mark at the end of the first paragraph if it ends with dialogue (as opposed to a dialogue tag or action beat). However, do put a quotation mark at the beginning of the second paragraph. Close with quotation marks only when the character has finished speaking. For example—

"I've been traveling for nearly two months," Jerry said, "and it's been an insightful journey. I've seen mountains and valleys, gorgeous trees and flowers.

"However, my travels have also taken me to some of the darkest places in our history."

XIX

And Then We Learned About Then

Then is an adverb. It is also a conjunctive adverb. Most importantly, then is *not* a coordinating conjunction.

When a conjunctive adverb separates two independent clauses, it is preceded by a semicolon and followed by a comma. Most people are aware of this rule when using such conjunctive adverbs as however and nevertheless.

Mom and Dad are traveling to Australia; however, they are taking a boat, not a plane.

Then, when separating two independent clauses, must be punctuated the same way.

Molly will be home from school at ten; then, the whole family will go to Grandma's house.

When used in other ways, a conjunctive adverb is sometimes set off by commas.

The accused, however, maintains his innocence.

Nevertheless, we will attend the party together.

And sometimes not.

He didn't study and consequently failed the test.

Then is often incorrectly used as a coordinating conjunction. This happens so frequently that it is often overlooked because it usually flows well and makes sense. Bear in mind, though, that the main reason incorrect usage begins to sound correct is because we get used to seeing and hearing it incorrectly. I suggest doing a search for "then" and eliminating every other one. Then, (notice correct usage) make sure the remaining "thens" are used correctly.

Incorrect—

He played baseball then took a shower.

He played baseball, then took a shower.

Correct—

He played baseball and took a shower.

He played baseball and then took a shower.

XX

Point of View Who?

My name is Helen, and I'm a point of view purist.

It's true. I stick to one character's point of view (POV) in every scene I write, and I resist having that character surmise about other characters' thoughts and actions. I do the same when I'm editing, and I've had more than one author fight me on it.

"But that's his perception of what is going on!"

Perception is okay, but remember that you're the author, not the character, and as such, you are all-knowing. Consequently, your character might be perceiving something that a normal person would not perceive in that instance. Much more effective ways exist to show a non-POV character's thoughts—dialogue and action, to name the two most important.

POV is a tough one for a lot of authors to master, but once you understand each type and its rules, it gets easier.

Third Person Limited

Most books are written in third person POV. This means the story is told from one character's viewpoint and written in third person, using the pronouns "he" or "she." The point of view may change to another character in another chapter or scene, depending on the story's needs. The writer is limited to what the viewpoint character knows.

If, for story reasons, the POV must change in a scene, it should change only once mid-scene. The transition must be clear and the read must not be disrupted. I personally recommend sticking to one POV per scene.

Head hopping (switching POV every couple lines or paragraphs) is disorienting to a reader, and most publishers frown on it. Yes, some best-selling authors (who shall remain nameless) head hop, but mere mortals like the rest of us really shouldn't. Let me put it this way. An editor may reject your manuscript for head hopping, but no editor will ever reject you because you didn't head hop. He may reject, but lack of head hopping won't be the reason.

First Person

First person POV is written from one character's viewpoint and uses the pronoun "I." First person has become quite popular in the last decade. Some authors use multiple first person POV, switching characters every chapter.

Second Person

This type of POV uses the pronoun "you." I'm using second person in this book to refer to you, the reader. Second person is uncommon in fiction. If you're familiar with the novel *Bright Lights, Big City* by Jay McInerney (which spawned the movie of the same name, starring Michael J. Fox), you know it was written in second person. I've also seen it used in erotica recently. But all in all, it's quite rare.

However, what is not rare is for an author writing in third person to inadvertently slide into second person from time to time, completely unaware that he has done so. I'm sure you've seen it. You're reading along, and you find a sentence like this.

Jack knew one of the benefits of having a girlfriend was **you** *always had a date for dances.*

These shifts into second person are distracting and should always be corrected. Fortunately, it's usually an easy fix.

Omniscient

Omniscient POV is told by an all-knowing narrator. Though written in third person, omniscient POV allows the narrator to see into any character's thoughts and to reveal past or future events. Limited omniscient means the narrator is only in one character's head at a time, but he still has his crystal ball and can see things the character cannot.

Omniscient POV has fallen out of favor in modern writing. It's now usually only seen in epic novels. I don't recommend it. Unless omniscient POV is executed with masterful technique, it can weaken a story and dilute the reader's allegiance to any single character.

New writers sometimes slip into omniscient POV without knowing it. For example, consider the following sentence, written from the woman's viewpoint.

When Jack gazed in her direction, Myra's cheeks turned crimson.

Is Myra looking in a mirror? Probably not, since she sees Jack looking at her. The problem is that Myra can't see her cheeks, so she has no idea whether they're crimson or not. However, she can feel them. This is an easy fix.

When Jack gazed in her direction, Myra's cheeks warmed.

Stick to what your POV character can see, hear, feel, taste, smell, or reasonably surmise, but keep surmising to a minimum. It's much more effective to show non-POV characters' thoughts through their actions and dialogue than to have the POV character constantly assuming what they're thinking or why they're doing something.

XXI

A Participial Phrase is not a Gerund

Often the two are confused. A gerund is a present participle that functions as a noun.

Running is my favorite activity.

A participial phrase begins with a present or past participle. If the participle is present, it will end in -ing. A regular past participle will end in -ed. Irregular past participles end in all kinds of ways.

Participial phrases always function as adjectives.

Shouting with happiness, Laurie celebrated her promotion.

Glazed with hoisin sauce, the ribs looked delectable.

Use participial phrases sparingly. Action verbs are usually much stronger.

Correct— *Brushing her hair, she smiled in the mirror.*

Better— *She brushed her hair and smiled in the mirror.*

Participial phrases denote concurrency, so be careful not to write a sentence that results in impossible simultaneous actions.

Running toward the house, she opened the door and entered.

She can't be running toward the house and opening the door at the same time, but that is what this sentence says. Rewrite the sentence.

She ran toward the house, opened the door, and entered.

Caveat— Make sure the participial phrase modifies the subject of the sentence. Otherwise it will result in a dangling modifier.

XXII

I Felt My Heart Flutter

That's filtering.

Filtering is a common style problem that I see all the time in published writing. It occurs when the writer "filters" imagery or action through the senses of the POV character. This distances the reader from the story by creating an extra layer between the reader and the event. The reader then, instead of being in the story and witnessing what is happening, is knocked outside the story and is told what is happening. Filtering turns a show into a tell.

Take a look at my chapter heading. You've no doubt read similar sentences.

I felt my heart flutter.

Well, yes, if my heart fluttered, I no doubt felt it. But is it necessary to say that if I'm writing about it? Of course not. It's much more effective to say:

My heart fluttered.

I've cut out the filtering middleman and simply shown my fluttering heart.

Most authors don't realize they're filtering. Fortunately, doing a search of the most common filtering verbs will highlight most filtering. Once you become aware of filtering, it will start to stick out at you and you'll begin avoiding it.

Common filtering verbs—

decide

experience

feel

hear

imagine

know

look

notice

realize

see

seem

sound

think

touch

watch

wonder

Filtering— *She saw her mother drive away.*

Correction— *Her mother drove away.*

Filtering— *He realized that the lock had been picked.*

Correction— *The lock had been picked.*

Caveat— These filtering verbs can also be *action* verbs. Consider the following two sentences.

She saw her mother.

She saw her mother drive away.

In the first sentence, "saw" defines the action in the sentence. This is not filtering.

In the second, "saw" is a filtering verb; the action is her mother driving away. Since we're in "her" POV, no reason exists to tell the reader that she saw her mother driving away. Simply show her driving away.

XXIII

The Curious Case of the Traveling Fingers

Surely you've read a sentence like this.

His fingers traveled up her thigh.

Did his fingers detach and travel up her thigh? Of course not. Sentient body parts are a common problem in writing style. Body parts cannot move by themselves. The character, not the body part, produces the action.

Incorrect— *His hand stroked her cheek.*

Correct— *He stroked her cheek.*

Sometimes it's okay to use sentient body parts for a non-POV character if that is how the POV character perceives it happening. For example, if your POV character's eyes are closed and she feels "his fingers traveling up her arm."

But for the most part, please keep your body parts attached.

XXIV

Don't Tell Me the Moon is Shining; Show Me the Glint of Light upon Broken Glass

I wish I could take credit for that quote; it's one of my favorites. Alas, it belongs to Anton Chekhov, a Russian author whom I first read when I took a Russian literature course in college. To me, this quote perfectly explains—*shows*—the difference between "telling" and "showing" in writing.

Consider the following two first lines.

It was a dark and stormy night.

From *Paul Clifford* by Edward Bulwer-Lytton, in the public domain.

Night gripped the city with cold, misty darkness.

From *Shanna* by Kathleen E. Woodiwiss, copyright 1977.

"It was a dark and stormy night" has become the poster child for bad first lines. Madeleine L'Engle used it in her Newbery Medal-winning young adult masterpiece, *A Wrinkle in Time*, most likely as a joke. The line is all telling.

Compare it to Ms. Woodiwiss's first line. Both lines describe the same type of night, but which speaks to you more? The second one shows the stormy night, immerses you into it, and the misty darkness envelops you as you begin to read her story.

Showing gets easier with time and practice. Here are five ways to help you show, rather than tell, your story. Master these five and you should become a showing machine!

Deep Point of View

Deep POV is exactly what it sounds like: going so deep into the character that the author no longer exists. Only the character and her thoughts, words, actions exist, and the reader slides into her skin and becomes her. If your character gets chills, your reader gets chills. And you, as the author, probably got chills when you wrote it.

Take a look at the following two paragraphs.

Excerpt one—

Jane listened to Chandler's angry piano playing. Still holding the pot, she stood as he pounded on the grand piano. The notes were discordant, but she understood them. He looked tense, and he was sweating. The music got softer, and then louder, slower, and then faster. Jane continued to listen to the terrifying music, her heart racing, until he suddenly stopped.

Excerpt two—

The music called to her. His anger, his passion, called to her. Still holding the pot, Jane stood, mouth agape, as Chandler pounded out disharmonic chords on his nine-foot black lacquer grand. Disharmonic, yes, but they made a certain musical sense. Discordant in a harmonic way.

Sweat covered his brow and a drop hit an ivory key. He didn't stop to wipe away the perspiration. He punished the keys, ground out eerie yet beautiful music in his raw madness. His fingers danced. His facial muscles tensed. His full pink lips pursed. Another drop of sweat hit a key as he slowed the tempo, softened his strokes, and then from piano to forte again as he trilled two notes and boomed through the lower keys.

Jane's heart thudded in time with Chandler's now increasing tempo. As he crescendoed, so did she, her breath coming in rapid puffs, her breasts heaving against her chest. His playing conjured images in her mind of a bullfighter twirling a red cape. Vivid reds and oranges swirled through her head. More chords. Louder, faster…banging, clashing…

Then…silence.

From *Pianist Envy*, copyright 2011 by Helen Hardt.

Which one immersed you into the scene? Excerpt two, I hope. That's deep POV. Can you hear the pounding? The clashing chords? Can you feel Jane's heart thudding in time with the music? Her breath catching? Can you see the perspiration on Chandler's forehead? Can you imagine the twirling bullfighter? Jane's whole world became Chandler's music, and her body reacted to it in a visceral way. Deep POV keeps the intensity high and pulls the reader into the character's skin.

Should you write a whole novel this way? Probably not. But when a certain scene calls out for intensity, try deep POV. It's a very effective way of "showing" and forcing your reader into the moment.

Dialogue

When written well, dialogue is fun to read and is the ultimate way to "show" a story. It builds characterization as well. Your readers learn the most about your characters through their dialogue and interaction with others in the story.

Your dialogue must be realistic, but remember that there is a fine line between mimicking real conversation and copying it. No one wants to read a conversation full of "er," "um," and "you know," even though that's how people sometimes talk. Don't be afraid to use fragments or cut off sentences when they work to further the scene, but for the most part, your dialogue should be written in complete sentences. Use contractions; that's how people talk. Reading your dialogue aloud is an effective tool for making sure it sounds realistic and not stilted.

If you find several paragraphs of narrative in your manuscript, try to rewrite some of it into dialogue. Perhaps your character is walking down the street looking into windows and describing what he sees. Instead, have a shop owner notice him, come out to the sidewalk, and ask him if he'd like to see the gold ring he's eyeing. Or have a friend walk by and say hello and ask him what he's doing. He can then say he's looking for a gift for his girlfriend, for example.

Don't forget internal dialogue. This is an amazing tool for showing, and it's good for deep POV as well. Consider the following.

Paragraph one—

He felt nervous as he looked around the room for her. He chewed on his lip. She was there, standing alone in the corner.

Paragraph two—

Why did I come here? He breathed harder. Would she even be here? He bit his lip and gazed around the room. His heart jolted. She stood in the corner, alone. *Guess it's now or never.*

Internal dialogue pulls the reader right into the scene and into the character.

Say No to Labeling

Resist the temptation to label emotions and expression instead of showing them from the POV character's perspective.

Telling— *She looked at him curiously.*

Showing— *She lifted her eyebrows and widened her eyes.*

Be specific, rather than vague.

Vague— *She felt happy.*

Specific— *Elation filled her, and she smiled.*

What emotion is your character feeling? Now, think about what a person looks like when he's feeling that emotion, and simply show what you see. If it's the POV character, show also what he's feeling inside.

Action and Imagery

Our language is full of descriptive nouns and verbs, yet I'm amazed how many authors still rely on the old standbys like come, go, do, put, make, like, pull, have, run…the list goes on and on.

Take a look at my paragraph from *Pianist Envy* above. Here are some of the descriptive verbs I used.

pounded

punished

danced

tensed

softened

trilled

boomed

shuddered

crescendoed (and I'm not sure this is actually a verb, but hey, creative license) conjured

swirled

Make your thesaurus your best friend. When I write, I keep an online thesaurus open. When I need an effective noun, adjective, or verb, but all I can think of is "put" or "happy," I plug it in and go from there. If I don't find what I want, I click on one of the responses and continue until I find the perfect word. It's always out there.

Seize the Moment with Sensory Detail

No matter what time of the year it is, when I smell the yeasty, citrusy aroma of my mother's homemade raisin bread, I'm instantly transported back to my childhood holidays in Ohio. Raisin bread was a Christmas tradition. My mother made a gargantuan blob of dough speckled with light and dark raisins and laced with oil of lemon. She separated the dough into myriad little pieces and braided them into loaves. Then into the oven they went, and the glorious scent wafted through the house for the next several days.

Our senses make memories. In a story, sensory detail does the same thing. As your character experiences an event through his senses, so does your reader. And if you do your job well, your reader will remember that detail for a long time, and hopefully will seek out more of your books for a similar experience.

Sensory detail is extremely important in fiction writing. The reader wants to see, hear, smell, taste, and feel (and I'm not just talking sense of touch here, I mean inner feelings, as well) everything the characters do.

Not to get too technical on you, but "sensory," as defined, means "conveying nerve impulses from the sense organs to the nerve centers." As writers, we need to go beyond labeling feelings and emotion, even beyond describing them. We need to become our POV character, feel what he or she feels, see what he or she sees, etc. Then we translate those feelings—those nerve impulses—into words. When you master sensory detail, your scenes will be urgent, in the moment, and very powerful.

Easier said than done, right? Actually, it's not that difficult, and with a little practice, your scenes will shine with new color and vibrancy. No passive voice allowed! Keep adverbs to a minimum, but don't be afraid to use them if they work for the scene. Adjectives are essential, especially for describing scents. While description is a good start, use other tools—action, dialogue, imagery, similes/metaphors, to name a few—to convey feelings through words.

When you create each scene, ask yourself what each character is feeling. What does she see? Hear? Taste? Smell? What does she feel beneath her fingers? Against her body? What is she thinking? How is her body physically reacting to any stimuli? How is she emotionally reacting? Answer these questions, and then work the answers into the scene in the most vivid way possible. Don't forget your non-POV character. Work his senses into the scene through dialogue and actions.

Be careful not to overdo it. Ornate prose can be beautiful, but too much of it becomes a little tedious. How many times have you skimmed through a paragraph description that includes descriptions like "the inky blackness of the misty night illuminated by the silky gossamer moonlight cascading over the rippling waves of the pond"? A sentence or two is okay, but a whole paragraph or scene of this? You want to keep your reader immersed and entertained, not make him sick.

Sometimes a scene lends itself more to one sense than another. In my example below, you'll see I only use the sense of smell once. I've written many other scenes where I focus more on that sense. Be true to your characters and your story, and the senses will fall into place.

Here's the first kiss from *The Outlaw's Angel*, copyright 2012, Helen Hardt.

Looking into Naomi's glaring eyes, Bobby lost all rational thought. He seized her upper arms, pulled her to him, and crushed his mouth to hers.

Her full red lips were as sweet as he'd imagined. He nibbled across the upper, and then the lower, tasting the remnants of the raspberries she'd eaten with her supper. Sweet, tangy, and oh so perfect. He cherished each second of the kiss, knowing she'd break away at any time. Probably slap him across the face. It'd be no less than he deserved.

Instead, she wove her arms around his neck and whispered against his mouth, her voice a sensual caress.

"Bobby."

His name. How sweet the sound from her innocent lips. He was a goner now. His cock woke in his britches, and he pulled her against his arousal.

"Open, angel," he said against her rosebud mouth. "Open your lips, and let me in."

"I don't know how..." She broke away and spoke into his chin. At the same time she entwined her fingers in his hair. "Bobby. This isn't...proper."

"To hell with proper, darlin'. Kiss me back. Please. I'm aching for you." He found her mouth again and drank from her raspberry lips. "Open. Please."

A soft sigh escaped her throat as she parted her lips, just a touch, and he slipped his tongue between them. Every nerve in his body screamed for him to thrust into her mouth, to mimic what he wanted to do with another part of his body. But he held himself in check. Likely, she'd never kissed a man before, and even if she had, she was otherwise untouched. As much as he wanted her, he didn't want to scare her away.

But when the tip of her sweet tongue touched his, he shattered. He pulled her closer, and reached behind her with one hand and began plucking out those dratted hairpins. His other hand held her back at the waist, pulling her against the throbbing in his groin. Soon his fingers were tunneling through the thick sable waves. They were softer than he'd imagined, like fine oriental silk. A throaty groan rumbled from her chest, and like the waters through a dam breaking, he rushed forward, thrusting into her satiny mouth with urgent, yet tender, kisses. His tongue tangled with hers, and when she moaned again, he deepened the kiss, tasting every crevice of her soft, sweet mouth.

The kiss went on and on, and when she finally broke away, her breath came in rapid puffs against his cheek.

"Angel," he whispered, "you're so beautiful. So perfect." He rained kisses across her cheek, her jaw line, to the tender spot below her earlobe. Her lavender fragrance ensnared him, and he inhaled deeply. Still she panted against him, and he waited for her to stop him, almost

wanted her to stop him, because if he didn't stop soon, he wasn't sure he'd be able to.

"Bobby." Desire thickened her voice.

But he couldn't do this.

She was too good for the likes of him. To soil her would be to bastardize perfection. Once more, though. Just one more taste of those honeyed lips, and then he'd stop. He nibbled at her neck, breathing in her lavender essence, and then trailed to her lips again.

"Naomi," he said, and bent to touch his mouth to hers.

She gasped, but before he could thrust his tongue into her, she broke away from him, turned, and ran toward the creek.

Who'd he been trying to kid? If he'd tasted her again, he wouldn't have been able to stop.

I did something different with this scene. The first kiss is in the hero's point of view. That's not the norm for me, but it allowed me to focus on different details.

Let's take a look at the sensory detail.

First, the sense of sight. What is Bobby seeing during the kiss? Well, not a lot. Most people close their eyes when they kiss. But first, he sees Naomi's glaring eyes. Later, he imagines her ruby lips, her creamy thighs. Using the sense of sight for images in the mind is a great way to bring it into a kiss.

Let's move to smell. Mostly just her lavender fragrance.

How about hearing? Lots to work with there. The sound of his name from her innocent lips. Her soft sigh, her throaty groan. He hears desire thickening her voice. Can you hear it? I can.

Taste? This is a good one for kissing. Bobby tastes the remnants of the raspberries Naomi ate with her supper. It's a sweet and tangy flavor. He refers to her lips as "honeyed." Again, sweetness.

Last, but not least, the sense of touch, which includes inner feeling. This is the biggie. Most of your sensory detail will come from this sense. What does your character feel as he's caressing the other character? What does he feel inside, both physically and emotionally? Let's look to Bobby.

First, he seizes her and crushes his mouth to hers. This shows more emotion that just saying he pulled her into his embrace and kissed her, doesn't it? He cherishes the kiss, because he expects her to stop him. When Naomi whispers against his neck, her voice is a sensual caress. He gets an erection and pulls her against it. He tangles his hands in her hair, and it feels like soft Oriental silk. He feels her puffs of breath against his cheek. Inside, his body is screaming for him to thrust into her, to mimic the sex act. He knows she's inexperienced, so he holds himself in check for as long as he can. Can you feel his need? His desire? His conscience gets to him, but just one more kiss, he thinks. When she flees, he knows the truth. He wouldn't have been able to stop at one more kiss.

Can you feel the urgency? Not just for Bobby, but for Naomi as well? Her actions and words help impart her own emotions into the scene.

Although I used a love scene as an example, sensory detail adds depth to any scene. Show what your character is sensing, and your scene will come alive.

XXV

Miscellaneous Miscellany

"Alright" is not a word. This spelling is not recognized by *Merriam-Webster* or *The Chicago Manual of Style*. The correct spelling is "all right."

Use "sneaked" instead of "snuck" as the past tense of sneak. "Snuck," while considered correct, is nonstandard.

Use "dived" instead of "dove" as the past tense of dive. "Dove," while considered correct, is nonstandard.

The past tense of "to plead" is "pleaded," not "pled."

Use "farther" for physically measurable distances. Use "further" for nonphysical distances or "to a degree."

You are "racked" with pain, or you "rack" your brain. You are not "wracked" with pain. "Wrack" means "to wreck."

You "riffle" through your drawer looking for something. If you "rifle" through a drawer, you have the intent to steal something.

"Myriad" is an adjective, not a noun. You have myriad ideas. You do not have "a myriad of" ideas.

"Awhile" means "for a while." "A while" is much more common and should always be used if a preposition is present. Steer clear of "awhile" if you don't understand the difference.

"Blond" v. "blonde"— Always use "blond" as an adjective, regardless of the gender of the noun you're modifying. *She has blond hair.* As a noun, use "blonde" when the gender is female, "blond" when the gender is male. *The sexy blonde walked past me.*

"Irregardless" is now in the dictionary! Obviously no one called to ask my opinion on the matter. However, it is considered nonstandard. Please use "regardless."

XXVI

The Elusive Writer's Voice

My older son, Eric, is a professional opera singer. He has a beautiful and rich bass-baritone, and everyone comments on it.

He began his musical endeavors at age six with piano. He excelled, but as he got to the higher levels, he wasn't content to simply play the notes on the page, and though he often placed in competitions, he rarely won. Instead, the judges chose the competitor who played the piece perfectly and robotically as written. My son would tweak it here and there and add emotion. In other words, he made the piece his own. I always found the judges' choices odd, since the musicians who truly make their mark in the world are not the robots, but the individuals.

Though he still plays, singing is his passion now. After all, singing voices are unique, so he's allowed to be himself. When he was a studio artist for the Central City Opera in Colorado one summer, one of the professional vocalists said to him, "Eric, there's something really special about your voice." Clearly, the performer couldn't put into words what "special" was, but he was responding to my son's voice.

A writer's voice isn't a lot different. Editors will often pick manuscripts out of the slush pile because they respond to an author's voice.

But what is "voice?" For a singer, it's a little easier to define, but it does go beyond the vibrations made by the vocal cords. It's the expression of the individual himself through his vocal instrument.

Similarly, your writing voice is the expression of "you" in your work. It's not your impeccable grammar or your writing style. It's not your fondness for dialogue or first person point of view. But all of these and more contribute to your voice. It can be similar to the way you talk, or it can be completely different. Your attitude and your emotions are integral parts of your voice, and they will come across in your writing, but they alone will not define your voice. All of these things, plus myriad more, come together to make your unique writer's voice.

Clear as mud, right?

The concept becomes easier to grasp if you just think of your voice as an extension of you—of what makes you unique.

Your voice will evolve. You're not the same person you were ten years ago, and your voice will reflect that. Just as my son's singing voice has matured and grown through the years and will continue to develop as he studies and performs throughout his career, a writer's voice also grows. The more you write, the more defined your voice will become.

Your voice is all about you. Your experiences, thoughts, emotions—they will all shine through in your voice. Your voice may be similar to another author's, but it will never be identical.

Whether your voice appeals to others is subjective. Some will enjoy your voice; others may not. This is the way of the world. Don't let a negative review get you down—but you will anyway. We all do. Cry if you have to. Drink a glass of wine and eat some chocolate. Take solace in the fact that the most popular authors in the world have their share of negative reviews. And then move on. Never take your eyes off the prize.

As you work through the sections in this book, apply them to make your writing stronger. Don't worry that you're affecting your voice. You're not. You're honing your craft. Though related, your craft and your voice are two different concepts. Your craft is all that you've learned about writing through education and experience. Your voice is how *you* shine through your craft.

Don't be afraid to express who you truly are. Be yourself—and that is when you will find your unique voice.

Afterword

I often get asked what resources I recommend for authors. In case you're wondering, yes, I do own a copy of *The Chicago Manual of Style*. It's a bulky one thousand page tome, but sometimes it's the only place where I can find the answer I'm looking for. For everyday grammar questions, my favorite is *The Writer's Digest Grammar Desk Reference* by Gary Lutz and Diane Stevenson. It's much easier to navigate than *CMOS*, and it's very thorough. And of course every author should have the old standby, *The Elements of Style* by Strunk and White. Read it cover to cover. It'll only take you an hour, and I guarantee you'll learn something.

For craft, nothing beats *GMC: Goal, Motivation, and Conflict* by Debra Dixon. Another great classic is *Writing the Breakout Novel* by Donald Maass. For a more hands-on approach, try *Break into Fiction* by Mary Buckham and Dianna Love.

Need motivation? Read *No Plot? No Problem* by Chris Baty, the founder of National Novel Writing Month. You won't get a lot of instruction, but you will definitely get pumped to write.

Last but not least, sometimes guidance from other writers helps drive authors toward their goal.

My two favorite writing memoirs are *On Writing* by Stephen King and *Bird by Bird* by Anne Lamott. These books inform, empower, and entertain.

All set? Now go get some style!

Fiction by Helen Hardt

Follow Me Series:

Follow Me Darkly

Follow Me Under

Follow Me Always

Darkly

Wolfes of Manhattan

Rebel

Recluse

Runaway

Rake

Reckoning

Gems of Wolfe Island

Moonstone

Steel Brothers Saga:

Trilogy One—Talon and Jade

Craving

Obsession

Possession

Trilogy Two—Jonah and Melanie

Melt

Burn

Surrender

Trilogy Three—Ryan and Ruby

Shattered

Twisted

Unraveled

Trilogy Four—Bryce and Marjorie

Breathless

Ravenous

Insatiable

Trilogy Five—Brad and Daphne

Fate

Legacy

Descent

Trilogy Six—Dale and Ashley

Awakened

Cherished

Freed

Trilogy Seven—Donny and Callie

Spark

Flame

Blaze

Blood Bond Saga:

Unchained

Unhinged

Undaunted

Unmasked

Undefeated

Sex and the Season:

Lily and the Duke

Rose in Bloom

Lady Alexandra's Lover

Sophie's Voice

Temptation Saga:

Tempting Dusty

Teasing Annie

Taking Catie

Taming Angelina

Treasuring Amber

Trusting Sydney

Tantalizing Maria

PRAISE FOR HELEN HARDT'S FICTION

WOLFES OF MANHATTAN

"It's hot, it's intense, and the plot starts off thick and had me completely spellbound from page one."

~The Sassy Nerd Blog

"Helen Hardt…is a master at her craft."

~K. Ogburn, Amazon

"Move over Steel brothers… Rock is *everything!*"

~Barbara Conklin-Jaros, Amazon

"Helen has done it again. She winds you up and weaves a web of intrigue."

~Vicki Smith, Amazon

FOLLOW ME SERIES

"Hardt spins erotic gold..."

~*Publishers Weekly*

"22 Best Erotic Novels to Read"

~*Marie Claire* **Magazine**

"Intensely erotic and wildly emotional..."

~*New York Times* **bestselling author Lisa Renee Jones**

"With an edgy, enigmatic hero and loads of sexual tension, Helen Hardt's fast-paced Follow Me Darkly had me turning pages late into the night!"

~*New York Times* **bestselling author J. Kenner**

"Christian, Gideon, and now...Braden Black."

~**Books, Wine, and Besties**

"A tour de force where the reader will be pulled in as if they're being seduced by Braden

Black, taken for a wild ride, and left wanting more."

~*USA Today* Bestselling Author Julie Morgan

"Hot. Sexy. Intriguing. Page-Turner. Helen Hardt checks all the boxes with *Follow Me Darkly!*"

~International Bestselling Author Victoria Blue

STEEL BROTHERS SAGA

"*Craving* is the jaw-dropping book you *need* to read!"

~*New York Times* bestselling author Lisa Renee Jones

"Completely raw and addictive."

~#1 *New York Times* bestselling author Meredith Wild

"Talon has hit my top five list…up there next to Jamie Fraser and Gideon Cross."

~USA Today **bestselling author Angel Payne**

"Talon and Jade's instant chemistry heats up the pages..."

~RT Book Reviews

"Sorry Christian and Gideon, there's a new heartthrob for you to contend with. Meet Talon. Talon Steel."

~Booktopia

About the Author

#1 *New York Times*, #1 *USA Today*, and #1 *Wall Street Journal* bestselling author Helen Hardt's passion for the written word began with the books her mother read to her at bedtime. She wrote her first story at age six and hasn't stopped since. In addition to being an award-winning author of romantic fiction, she's a mother, an attorney, a black belt in Taekwondo, a grammar geek, an appreciator of fine red wine, and a lover of Ben and Jerry's ice cream. She writes from her home in Colorado, where she lives with her family. Helen loves to hear from readers.

Please sign up for her newsletter here:

http://www.helenhardt.com/signup

Visit her here:

http://www.helenhardt.com

www.ingramcontent.com/pod-product-compliance
Lightning Source LLC
Chambersburg PA
CBHW032115280326
41933CB00009B/847